PRAISE FOR *IRIDESCENT PIGEONS*

"The homing instincts in Candace Walsh's *Iridescent Pigeons* are unerring, each poem crafting a sure flight to quiet revelation. Braiding past and present, childhood and motherhood, and loss and love, Walsh's luminous, acutely observed collection is ultimately a song of praise, honoring the sensuous beauty of everyday life."

Debra Allbery, author of *Fimbul-Winter* and *Walking Distance*

~

"Candace Walsh's soulful, intimate, diction-rich poems span forms, eras, and musics to get down to the sources of this constant memory-flooded movement we call the present."

Anselm Berrigan, author of *Something for Everybody*

~

"Come for the influence of Virginia Woolf, stay for the 'Dogs and Their Lesbians'! Inventing new forms and reinvigorating old language, from the opening poem's index/list-form to homages to Gerard Manley Hopkins' sacred profane, to Sapphic stanzas, this collection of poems shows us hard-won love and quietly triumphant queer eros and joy. Walsh's poems vibrate with meter, rhythm, and the language of Romantic poets brought to 21st century relationships. There is music here, all kinds, and we are in good hands with a speaker who reminds herself who she is by 'scream-singing to the Pixies.'"

Margaret Ray, author of *Good Grief, the Ground*

~

AF097380

"Candace Walsh's poems are at once deeply serious and playful. I'm drawn to their voluptuous phrasing, their lexical condensations—the 'gray-rimmed . . . sapsoft secrets' of tree limbs—reminiscent of Gerard Manley Hopkins, most notably in her elegantly sensuous pastiche 'Bowed Beauty.' There are so many stunning images here, rendered with crystalline precision: 'a murmuration perch so dense / the barren tree seems leafed until the birds lift off at once.' Walsh's speakers are utterly bemused by human relationships, viewing them at times from alien distances: love as perceived by unmatched socks, by seaweed, by stray dogs. Her poems—intensely, warily—celebrate familial, platonic, and romantic bonds, even as they ponder vestiges of the trauma love can leave behind."

J. Allyn Rosser, author of *Foiled Again* and *Mimi's Trapeze*

~

"*Iridescent Pigeons* is a slender volume, but it is big as an entire library, full of love, familial love, queer romantic love, love of the great poems that came before, love of the world in which we live. There is a lyric grace that runs through all these poems. Walsh is preoccupied with the literary tradition, as seen in her references to Virginia Woolf, Gerard Manley Hopkins, and Elizabeth Bishop. She uses these references not as exercises but as playful springboards to make her own very unique insights about life. My favorite example is her riff on Bishop's 'One Art.' There is much to remember in this beautiful book, indeed, much to learn by heart."

Peter Waldor, winner of the National Jewish Book Award

~

"Innovative and breathtaking, Candace Walsh's *Iridescent Pigeons* torques traditional poetic forms to offer a queer perspective on love, relationships, and the everyday. For example, she uses the cento and Sapphic stanza, among other forms, to capture different lived experiences, which coalesce around the smallest details. Through these details, such as cracked eggs, a sugar bowl, and lemon balm, she invites her readers into different forms of intimacy. Just as a 'sphere . . . blooms blue-green from the moon,' each poem blooms with exquisite images, which provide alternate ways of understanding one's relationship to one's past, to others, and the world."

Shannon K. Winston, author of *The Girl Who Talked to Paintings*

Iridescent Pigeons

by
Candace Walsh

YELLOW ARROW
PUBLISHING
Baltimore, Maryland, USA

Iridescent Pigeons
Copyright © 2024 by Yellow Arrow Publishing
All rights reserved.

Library of Congress Control Number: 2024939960
ISBN (paperback): 979-8-9883176-3-0

Cover art by Anna Chotlos (annachotlos.com); cover design by Laura M. André. Overall design by Yellow Arrow Publishing. For more information, see yellowarrowpublishing.com.

To those who hold my hands and my heart.

TABLE OF CONTENTS

on loving midwestern women	3
Not Fell but Fall	5
Visiting My Son, Foreign Student	7
Things I Broke	9
Bowed Beauty	11
Still Life and Loss with Lemons	13
Wild and Frail and Beautiful	15
I Wandered Lonely as a Romantic Friend in the 21st Century	17
"I want to see you in the lamplight, in your emeralds."	21
S(k)in	23
Kin	25
The Weight	27
Heart Failure	31
Sapphic Stanza 1	33
Sapphic Stanza 2	35
Sapphic Stanza 3	37
Then Suddenly I Know	39
Honey, Nest	41
The Last Third, Denver to Santa Fe	43

Pruning Song	45
Innocence and Mercy	47
inside the lip	49
Poem by Two Odd Socks	51
And They Did (Love You), and You Did (Have Reason)	53
If the Wound Is How the Light Enters You, How Do You Heal?	57
Dogs and Their Lesbians	59
Love Poem for Laura #4, 2009	61
Acknowledgments	65
About the Author	69

Iridescent Pigeons

ON LOVING MIDWESTERN WOMEN

guessing vs. asking	contrast of her *guess what I would like* (breeze, sometimes sleet) with my *this is what I want* (noonday sun, thunderclap).
the quality of quiet	prairies. peachdown. moonlight.
the weather	could be worse. see *guessing vs. asking*.
food	unfussy. packed freezers. intent. root cellars. jarred summer.
conversation	everything and nothing mean something. or more than one thing. silence is the *three* that never makes *a crowd*. see *the quality of quiet*. see *the weather*.
lexicon of gazes	fecund.
public displays of affection	no.
walks	not through but among. being met and meeting. naming and greeting. see *the quality of quiet*. see *conversation*.
things mourned/honored	old friends from younger times, capers with. grandmothers. witnessed indiscretions. misperceptions of impoliteness. what matters to me.

love	dogs. taught me how to love dogs. synonym: *watch out for deer*. see *food*.
mothers	circumspect huggers. constant. see *love*. see *food*.
fathers	often pilots. see *mothers*. see *love*.
shade	what is not said. what is said with other words. see *lexicon of gazes*. see *the weather*.
longing	inarticulate yet redeemingly keen. prairies. peachdown. moonlight.

NOT FELL BUT FALL

The ease in which
I fell asleep
against her chest

as she felt
my head's weight
and the not-weight of my hair
as it fanned across her skin
and spilled into her underarms' dark silk.

> Childhood summers
> I would stand waist-deep
> within the gentled sea
> as if it were my vast and rippling skirt
> and sunlight my chemise.

> Below my feet
> a ballroom floor of glossy stones.
> I'd trace the seaweed flumes
> borne by brine
> fine-boned as hair
> of black and rust and aubergine.

Rootless seaweed drinks in riches
from the medium in which it floats
and wanders. How do oceans feel
about these languid vagabonds?

Against her skin I knew, I think,
how seaweed feels.
The sea must feel a thing like love.

VISITING MY SON, FOREIGN STUDENT

And by the time I arrived you were one with the city,
a gem so at home Graz's prongs set off your acclimatized lilt.
On my flight, attendants wore red suits, hose, and pumps,
vulva-shaped caps. They gave out red-sheathed earplugs and snacks.

In Vienna's train station, a man unspools autumn's iteration
over a billboard's summer alpine scene.
Circling past his ladder's feet:
a fantasy toy train and its soft clacks.

Before my train is due, I use the coin-entry toilet,
staring at the stall door's menu under plexi.
It shills HOT CHAMPIGNONS, DIVERSE FISCHE.
I plan to ask you if it's customary
to tempt the belly as the colon empties.

Spotted through the train window:
a yellow EICHBERG hut with a mushroom cap roof.
Trainman's lounge or troll's lair?
A younger, maiden me would disembark and flâne on a whim.
I'm far too keen to reunite with you,
tall and true, but bittersweetly foreign.

I could carry you the last time we were here.
My hips still know your weight notched in my waist,
your fingers at my neck light as love, your
nodding head's dense rest. Snail tracks
of your saliva on my chest.
The way I craved to shape your life into vignettes
as queued and sweet as pastel macarons
and failed and failed and failed, like when I tripped
over a sandbox edge in France while holding you,
sand-gouges in my knuckles and my knees,
your scratched-up nose and cheeks.

Your wails, my red-hot wish
to fire, shit-can, heave-ho, pink-slip, and sack myself
and hire a better one. But that was then. Time does it anyway,
tosses us to spin in ardent orbits
of grazing fingertips.

Before you bring me to the castle gardens
rich with apple trees and peacocks,
I give you a disk of red-foiled plane chocolate,
the word *Servus* debossed into its face:
two silky syllables the Romans used when reigning in this place
to summon captive subjects
like a maid's bell ringing twice. It now means
what seems today to be a motherhood of phrases,
all of these at once, blur-stacked like palimpsests:
hello, I am here for you, goodbye.

THINGS I BROKE

First marriage, on purpose.

Wine glasses, canaries of a certain coal mine.

The sugar bowl my mother made in arts & crafts to get a break
from me. An accident while sneaking sweetness. I masked
the shards and crystals with a towel. A sorry subterfuge,
but I was 3. She was sad but not angry, glad I didn't scar.

The boombox I dropped at surly 13
while climbing beach bluff steps.
Another accident. I'd carped about having to carry it,
yet wouldn't throw it. My dad didn't believe me,
looked at me and saw a mirror-me who would, and then I did.
I had to break that, too.

Hundreds of eggs. Thousands? Cracked into bowls.
Including a bloody lumpen one I swiftly scooped into the bin
while making cookies for a wedding spread. Not mine.

Hearts, mine and others. A tail lagging behind, a string of cans,
timeline of my types. Children I babysat's dads, poor saps.
My aspirational dates. The one who eschewed eschewing
her heterosexuality for me (and good for her). The times I dated
down. The reach. The ones quitting the States in a matter of weeks.

> Do I break my wife's too much? Does she break mine?
> Do we break them together
> by staying entwined?

> The route to love we sought
> was one of falling, two rocks tumbling
> into shine.

A windshield, with my body.

The habit of taking my chances, not looking both ways.

BOWED BEAUTY

After "Pied Beauty" by Gerard Manley Hopkins

Glory be to goddesses of heft –
  The plush, broad, soft, round, thick;
    Thighs that hoist, shudder, shake, sprawl;
The faméd, flimsy female frame leaves me bereft.
  Praise buxom calves and weeping-willow hips;
    Slight swooping-inward dimpled-navel middle: thrall.

I love her: curved, swelled, stacked, arched, sloping;
  Her satiation-slackened, hunger-unencumbered lips
    Allude to pleasures undeferred. I fall,
And soft she takes me in. Sly lusts so unaligned with life-denying:
    Praise them.

STILL LIFE AND LOSS WITH LEMONS

My cousin died yesterday—it could have been avoided
had the pharmacist not tipped the wrong pills into his bottle.

When I was 4, Michael's hands shampooed my hair
as I strained after the bottle with a plastic lemon cap.
He was the quiet one among a cloud of roguish siblings.

To make preserved lemons, I once twisted fruit loose
from a tree near my lover's late grandparents' driveway.
Citrus grove for lawn. Did they think about, burying root balls
by the dozen, how long these saplings would outlive them?

I split the lemons crosswise twice, packed salt into the creases,
and stuffed them in the jar until their blood became their brine.
When we returned to the house her parents would sell
6 months later, the lemons had transformed.
We tossed the silken pith with chicken parts,
baked it in the ancient creak-door oven 'til
the vacant house smell (gas and ghosts) swelled
with piquant perfumes of the sun.

Today in grief and faith in mealtimes 6 months out
from Michael's death, I press store-bought
lemon sections into salt-strewn water.
Errant bursts of juice will leave the counter sticky.
Scattered salt will serve me as I scour it down to bone.

WILD AND FRAIL AND BEAUTIFUL

A cento (source Jacob's Room *by Virginia Woolf)*

something which can never be conveyed

uneven white mists
queer movements
chequered darkness

something in the room

yellow blinds and pink blinds
pink and yellow lengths of paper roses

something that would see them through

a tremulous haze
an eighteenth-century rain

something about being sure

the oval tea-table
the mustard on the tablecloth

something flying fast

iridescent pigeons
cloudy future flocks
a peacock butterfly

something whispers

a collection of birds' eggs
green wineglasses

something must be said

violets for sale
the violet roots and the nettle roots

    something silver on her arm

small smooth coins
sea glass in a saucer

    something for them

the flamingo hours
the worn voices of clocks

    something like selfishness

the pale blue envelope
the soft, swift syllables

    something very wonderful   has happened

I WANDERED LONELY AS A ROMANTIC FRIEND IN THE 21ST CENTURY

After William Wordsworth

As I, a bark with dogs for tugboats, walked
I passed a hillock humped from grassy ground
a few feet from the pebbled road its bed.

The mound was three feet wide, and sixish long,
a fence with drooping wires beside it wandered,
while grizzled grasses rasped the wind's pale song
and rusted posts aslant through breezes canted.

Three hills precede this bumptious eminence
concatenating stretches curve like hips
of giant maidens dozing on the sedge
with vine-bound tresses, honeysuckle breath

This road is ever yours and mine, I venture
two in a long line of familiars
who wandered out before us and shall after.

This lane bestows charms slow-revealed to those
who do not shirk from hills and swerves and barks
(modest the road's beginning is, and mounded
as if to repel fanciers of the flat-grounded).

Goats' doméd pates and smiling iris eyes
shambolic bouclé sheep so loosely swarmed
and lambs too young to doubt, their wool
a clotted cream for fingertips to dream
and tails that hang as limp as rodent prizes
a cat would bring its master uninvited.
Ears cocked like downy spoons of sounds:
our soles on gravel-spattered ground,
our words, the silences between

like dulcet lulls of corduroy.
A chainéd bull, three cud-caressing cows.
A dog's low larynx murder-murmur, shushed.

One early summer day before you left,
the hillock was awash in shrubby leaves
oft topped with daffodils, but not.
Perhaps it was a grave, instilled with bulbs
that propagate, return. A paean to grief
in their innate deadheaded form.

Your leaving was a kind of death,
stilling the weaving of a cloak
our souls' hands still soft in the making.
And so, bereft, I failed to walk so often or so far,
undone by slackened recent keenest need
without the mossy hushes of our thoughts
in which restraint inspiraled sly and slender-belled.

The hillock-tendrils shriveled. The ache permitted soothing,
there's mercy in the fading. And salve in this unearthing:
Connections from a distance hold a sweetness certain.

The dogs at least were sanguine in your absence,
I vigilant of tick-carbuncled grass
and keen to spare all dreamy creatures creeping
from jaw-snap-shake, then stillness scarlet-seeping.
To let the deer both singular and plural
lollop across the lane as canine bloodlust,
merely a scent, blurred quickly to irrelevance.

While when the dogs press snout to tracks of sylvan bounders,
they strain for more like ears of shackled sailors
affixed to masts of ships they pledged to shepherd into ports
before the spell transformed them,

to oaths and pledges, strangers;
transplanted truths and innocent deceivers.
The only cures:
wind in sails
bound limbs
distance gained
senses dulled.

Desire it is, the heat of friction felt
to follow the free, spine-dive and scratch,
worry the deer-slept beds with nose and tongue,
keen to leave one's stain / be stained,
even in absence of the quarry's pulse
(*smell-taste-touch*), the flame.

The summer neared its ending. No, let's call it
furlough, respite, intermission.
I passed the oblong mound of earth, stopped short
to see its body cloaked in scores
of silver-pink petaled lilies gleaming, unbothered
by their leafless stems—no, more than that—
insouciant, elated. Their yellow centers mad
with pistils luring bees and butterflies. And me.

And then you sent a photograph of these same blooms
with mouths like tiny suns or happy panting dogs
bunch-flung along a distant road where you continue
noticing, unfolding, breathing.

Again we were one, paired by the sight
like mushrooms springing from the same mycelial net;
glinting within the beats
of distant forests' hearts.

And so the redeeming lesson longing wrought:
To hell with the illusion of *apart*.
To hell with the myth of distance begetting endings.

"I WANT TO SEE YOU IN THE LAMPLIGHT, IN YOUR EMERALDS."*

I want to touch you
in the mottled dawnlight
mist of larkspur shadow
pressed thin

touch you I cannot
so this wind-rode air I yoke
noting the pang
as dawndusk floods my cells
as toll

pine: to wed with bouclé bark
and green too dense to fall
just emerald at its crest
sun-spored where far too fine
the ballast of my grasp
to nest

---

* The title of this poem is a sentence from a love letter Virginia Woolf wrote to Vita Sackville-West in 1927.

S(K)IN

I could no longer watch my dad get dressed for work
when I turned 4, a birthday banishment
that made his body wrong, made me wrong, too,
my pleas to keep my keen post on their bed

where I watched him walk, I watched things swing,
rose tones and umber fuzz, paperwhite skin
and the rest of him, of course, the rest of him.
He worked all night and slept all day
and this was—had been—my only time with him.

At 6 I made a neighbor friend named Sven.
His mom invited me to come on in.
I passed his father shaving in the open-doorway can:
biscuit cheeks, earthcurve paunch, ruddy prick,
plump biceps. Clothes-on grin.
Coffee cup balanced on the sink rim,
no big deal, no big thing.

My father's murky answers didn't put me off
from sliding on the sly beneath their quilt.
Breathpulse. No light. I would claim what was mine.

Time. He didn't have to know. I didn't need to see.
Just be. Near him. Mom sat. They talked. They laughed.
I laughed, lulled into thinking my ban had been a fluke.

Blinking in the bright
I was small as a tick ripped off a dog teat,
big enough to toss like a bag of soil,
no longer kin to him, but kin
to a malignance he was careful not to name
but quick to shun. And all this pain
because of love.

KIN

There are so many Walshes,
making strange the bonds of kin.
Maybe that's why we don't cling.

You, missing cousin, once called me your twin.
My mother claims I had our grandfather's favor
but you got his blue eyes and side-wind grin.

When I asked my mother about you,
she first talked about your mother's mother,
who kept a masturbating monkey in a cage.

Tell me your secrets, Melissa. How do you relate to men?
Our fathers—brothers—both withdrew.
But differently, as brothers do.

Post-divorce your mother got you
like a breakfront or a mirror. Entire.
The art of losing isn't hard to master.

I fall in love with
and mostly work for women.
One can at least—at last—succeed

while succeeding at avoiding
heartbreak fronts and foxed mirrors in the form of men.
And yet my son nears 20. What then?

Your father fought for you but caved in.
My father calls me, but only on Christmas,
taking his finger out of the dam
for 15 minutes.

THE WEIGHT

I've been thinking about the strength of trees.
We know roots hold earth like hundreds of handclasps—claps;
the wind's effects evoke a tantric dance.

The weight trees brook in forms of a fat bear on a branch
or thousands of birds, a murmuration perch so dense
the barren tree seems leafed until the birds lift off at once—
are burdens borne as strength.

But ice stitches this arms-wide tree,
turns branches to toothpicks—snap
gray-rimmed raw branch stumps—shock
sapsoft secrets—out.

Limbfall below the tree arranged
by chance? to supplicate—suggest
I strike a sibling-saving match.

HEART FAILURE

When your daughter wanted to hear you say
I'm proud of you,
you said,
You want intimacy.

Intimacy should be a given.
Pride in her should be an impulse,

a homing pigeon seeking,
not thinking. So many messages coiled
in its twig-slender cylinder.
So many places to land.

SAPPHIC STANZA 1

Chicory and acorns, flickering candle

Cyclamen and muslin and windswept violets

Silken locks and sable glances foment a

glittering madness

SAPPHIC STANZA 2

Sunlight on your dimple, routing its shadow.

Russet strands brush shoulders and tongue-traced hollows.

Fingers weave as footsteps echo. Walking as

lovers becomes us.

SAPPHIC STANZA 3

Dinosaur egg rocks, clefts, and declivities.

Virga daubs sky over mesa achingly.

Acid-green lichen. I long to be the sun's

last rake through your hair.

THEN SUDDENLY I KNOW

I let the helichrysum overtake its raised bed
because I love its name in my mouth—
(*helios chrysos*, sun gold)
after benign-neglecting the other bed
back into frenzies of mint, lemon balm, and bees.

When we planted two summers ago,
you showed me how to turn earth.

We pulled out pillow heaps of peppy mint
and soporific balm, but kept a swarm
for lemonade and love
and tea and luck (and bees).

    They say the only way to get rid of mint is
    to set the whole bed on fire.

I am, I must admit,
a great deal in love
with the fixity of
your roots. My mother
moved us every year,
tending one garden only long enough
to realize she loved tomatoes.

When you go *home*-home
you help tend your parents' garden,
where beets blush your insides
and berry juices violet-dusk your hair.

    They say helichrysum (*immortelle*)
    should not be harvested for magic use
    with garden tools or hands, but teeth.

Sometimes when I wake to pee at 3 a.m.
there seem to be many potential routes
to bathrooms of my youth:
the one with white penny tile and black grout
the one with floral foil wallpaper and green porcelain.
Then suddenly I know: turn left,
go down the stairs, through the kitchen, left,
then right.

> Somewhere because of us
> there are honeycombs dripping
> with lemony mint-lashed gold
> just for bees.

Sometimes I can't get back to sleep,
while lemon balm breathes
let me soothe you beyond the window screen
and frogsong trembles webs seedpearled with dew.

In my dark bed I lie entwined
in my vegetable love for you
beneath a minty balmy canopy
of Icarus vines be-domed,
impelled by their lust for *helios*
to soar up and fall back to earth—

but soft, but safe.

HONEY, NEST

I was the broken honey
throat bite tongue tang

helve crank mouth pour
light-shot vat flight

blossom   sweetbomb   limbslackener
queen swell   burr bell   peal

add time. clouds occluded cataracted
add heat. clear cream careen

feverfew frost-lace
moss gaze   *ill lust tree us*

beak-weave tinsel and thread into dwelling bowl
notch into arbor-cleft   swoopgrass edifice

v-ing, stinging
avian   again   apian   again

bloodbloom bellwether
eggshell ministerings   stamen manystrings

fletched-pierced proving ground
I was the remembered nest

THE LAST THIRD, DENVER TO SANTA FE

The sky and I look down
at vulva mountain cleavings,
rumpled piñon foothills.

Sandbox of the nonbinary divine,
tufts and ridges evidence
of slapped clay, squeezed layercake mounds
abandoned after a time.

On the plane,
someone is pulling up personal thunder
from their lungs.

The sphere that blooms blue-green from the moon
gives fawn and white and creosote from here.
Smudged circles in the snow mark
horses training girls and dirt

and all I can think
as our planeshadow drapes I-25
is

I drank so much here

We land like a swan,
the plane
imparting the savagery
of making peace with gravity.

I'm gonna cry / don't cry

PRUNING SONG

Elegance is refusal
decreed Diana Vreeland
while dabbing her lobes with rouge.

I trim
back the bonsai,
I trim.
I count off 4 tea leaves and clip.

I tilt the aqua spindle-spout pitcher,
something a grandma would leave in her sunroom
with wind chimes, next to an ashtray
sponged out after every stubbed-out cigarette.

Imagine the power of all that growth lust
rammed back into existing shoots,
limbs, trunk, and roots.
Or, I don't have to.

I am waiting for these trees to bud
their slight white blooms
that wink like stars
removed from me by years of light.

Their scent will fill this room of my own;
on that I shall not stint.

INNOCENCE AND MERCY

My grandmother's neck pulsed with bobbles,
skin tags that waved when she moved.
She'd wait until ripeness
and then the dermatologist
would remove them in one fell harvest.

She was plump and wore polyester pantsuits
in colors of coral, swimming pool,
would bat away my toddler fingertips.

I recalled their warm braille
when I found a skin tag on my neck
and pinched it bloody off like lint.

When I was 13 or 12
I shaved the hair at the nape of my neck,
irked by spiraling baby hairs
like the ones between my legs.

I craved a clean line.

Then my mother caressed me, felt the stubble
at my now-thin grandmother's house.
I had done so many things to make my mother cry
but this was accidental.
Mercy came in the form of my grandmother's bemusement,
her calm amid my mother's mascara-flowing storm.

Last night my body woke me up again at 2 a.m.
steaming like a salmon beneath a silver dome.
If it's wintertime I go outside,
take off my shirt and stand in the dark backyard,
bare my trunk amid the soaring trees' rough bark,
let the flinty wind hit my skin like a million fingertips

that know exactly how I like to be touched.

There is a small mercy for every ill
and the best ones ask you to stand still,
do nothing to earn it
just take it.

INSIDE THE LIP

inside the lip of an indigo lake
in a red state
you showed me
your water ballet

POEM BY TWO ODD SOCKS

hanging from the laundry rack you use
because mice got into the dryer.

You're heating up the frozen soup
you made when your son was here.
He said it smelled bad
and wouldn't taste it.

The glass bowl cracked
sometime after you put
the too-hot into the too-cold and walked.

You only noticed now:
the fracture in a snake-sine wave.
Will you? Yes, you'll take your chances,
open to a mini shard of glass
grazing your insides. Penance.

We watched you let go of him slowly
and then all at once. Pain met youth's insouciance.
You found grace. Or it found you.

Or do you let go with undue haste?
We don't have our mates,
are rarely used. Do not protest too much.

Maybe if he'd tasted it he would have liked it
and there would be none left over
to warm your belly near the place
where out he once tadpoled from weary love.

(We're not judging you,
but at the end of the summer
you are a woman
who lets go of your son
but hangs onto odd socks.)

AND THEY DID (LOVE YOU), AND YOU DID (HAVE REASON)

If you are a writer, and
you will be ghosted by two friends for the first time since 8th grade,
make sure they're not the ones who mockingly read aloud
the published work of people they don't like.

You will find your mind has turned into a stray dog, as in lost
(although most stray dogs must identify as lost because
there must be some misunderstanding),
sniffing at the asses of countless was-it-thises-or-thats
and you must pull your mind back on its frayed rope leash
to all the good things you deserve to think about. But do you?
Maybe "no" is the big secret everybody knows and you don't.

Because ghosting is so junior high, as are the thoughts it churns up.
You could talk about it to your therapist more productively
if you hadn't sent one of those friends to her
because you were gravely worried about her wellbeing.

You've already deleted one friend's birthday playlist,
the one your wife made, and their recurring birthday reminders
from your phone calendars, and now understand
retrospectively why even though you threw them birthday parties
they kind of asked you to throw because of their birthday baggage
and baked their cakes,

that even though they were out of town on your birthdays,
it was fucked that they needed to be reminded to wish you
happy birthday, especially since the conversations
about birthday baggage included your own.
Until after they ghost, when the carelessness
will seem so intentional—not toward you;
toward edging out the back.

You would have more friends to fall back on
if you hadn't let certain friendships fade because one friend
didn't like them. You would have made more friends
if they hadn't been soaking up all your friend bandwidth
as you were throwing good money after bad, friendship-wise,
and didn't even know it, not just before they ghosted you,
but after, when the part of you that hopes, seeks the optimistic/
realistic take, like *there must be some misunderstanding*,
went *oh*
like an outbreath of balloon. *They're really gone.*

Are they really gone if one still has your pulse oximeter?
She must feel entitled to keep something you lent her
because you were gravely worried about her wellbeing.

It is time, time to buy a new thing
that measures the strength of your heart and breath
with a fingertip clasp. Then will they be gone?

As someone with a kite-high ACEs score, you're skilled at absolving
people only Christ could forgive (because it's His damn job).
But you've buffed those muscles to maintain relationships with kin
you can't opt out of loving; you've tried.

Were the friends to repent, they'd have had a story
a single you would opt to believe
for the sake of reweave. But because
they were also your wife's friends and their ghosting broke her heart
and made her cry, and still does, like when she sees
pictures of their dogs (you *named* one of them) on Instagram,
you want to waffle-stomp them through a sewer grate. You
who catch and release ladybugs on the porch where they
(not the bugs, the friends, the ex-) ran up so many times

with ice cream, or the big container of mixed greens,
or white tequila and a bag of limes, with their dogs,
and their hard-squeeze hugs hello
and goodbye (like the last one you didn't know—)
that said to your pocket of ACEs: This is real, you have no
reason to doubt us when we say
we love you

IF THE WOUND IS HOW THE LIGHT ENTERS YOU, HOW DO YOU HEAL?

Picture perforation in a pattern,
punch-out paths of constellations
dappling your bedroom ceiling
when love was a soft plump animal,
not a taloned thing.

Place clay coins over the wounds.
Let the sun suckle them dry,
pull the poison into poultice palms.
Peel off the earthen dusty husks.
Tap oil on the blinking scabs.
Wait.

Drop into a bowl of time:
      cherry pits
      every dozenth tear
      blooms that sprawl in sun
      a strand from her left-behind brush.

Remember how *mar* means flaw and also the sea
How *ding* means dent and also a peal
How *rupture* is the godmother of *rapture*
How *pain* is also bread.

DOGS AND THEIR LESBIANS

Sometimes when we come home,
Sadie wags her tail
so hard against the wall it bleeds.

The vet calls this "happy tail"
and quotes the price to cut it off.
I think of dogs with docked tails,
their bumpy rumps wagging nothing.

It reminds me of queer love,
how they used to try to
cut off or drug-numb what offended,
how we sniffed out the invisible
and guess-read the signals,
pretending to be cats, aloof and skittish
when we felt like dogs, ecstatic and lickish.
And when we could finally pounce,
how hot it surged,
or hardly stirred—so deeply stilled.
We know how much it costs
to cut it off. I'd rather clean up blood.

My ruptured love for runaway dogs, hit-by-a-car dogs,
given-away-to-folks-on-the-farm dogs
new-landlord-doesn't-allow dogs
marred my childhood.
I came to you with a calloused heart,
not a dog person per se.

You and your soon-to-be my dogs
sanded my heart down to softness
one lick at a time,
over time. Faithful, *fidel*, Fido:
I will stay with you.

Once after seeing a photo of you
taken 10 years before we met,
I felt the hindsight grief of life before you.
I ached to touch your long dark hair
(now short and silver-strewn) and say
Someday we will come home to us,
and Sadie will lie near our feet on the bed
and growl when we move,
then stalk off to her crate.
This will upset you every time,
as will any movies
where the dog gets hurt or worse.
I'll skip past those parts
while you sing in the next room
to block out traumatizing sounds.
I will clean up the blood.

Each time our dogs die from old age we think
we might stop adopting dogs
to keep from mourning them anon. But no,
we know how much it costs to cut it off,
although this love is messy
and will always bring back the ball, want more.

We go to sleep with blanket-hogging dogs.
And on our bedroom dresser rests
(along with socks with missing mates, a jar of change,
a silent music box, and dust)
a row of labeled floral tins of ashes.

One of the ways we say *good night* is
I will stay with you.

LOVE POEM FOR LAURA #4, 2009

Isn't it funny how
you had to nervously go
and meet a room of strangers tonight
who meet to get over their fear
of meeting strangers

when one year and one week ago
you had to nervously go to a restaurant
to meet me?

I was so nervous that night
I drove the hour down south
past tumbleweeds and wrecks
scream-singing to the Pixies
to remind myself who I was.

I learned that sometimes fear
entwines the best things
that ever happen to me.

I want to reach inside you
and turn your fear to ease.
I want your soul to hear
the way it hums
the way a mother
lulls her babe to sleep
and somehow calms me,
knits me to you,
stitches more each day.

you are my sunshine
you are my moonshine
you are my pearl
you are my flowering
you are my fallowing
you are my dove.

I will be here
a nest
a net
a simple truth
a kiss
a palimpsest
a promise.

You don't know the gift you are,
but I do.
And in the meantime,
you let me open you.
You let me hold you.

ACKNOWLEDGMENTS

HAD (online), November 2021
"on loving midwestern women"

Lovers Literary Journal, March 2022
"Sapphic Stanza 1"

Beyond Queer Words, spring 2022
"If the Wound Is How the Light Enters You, How Do You Heal?"

Husk, spring 2022
"Not Fell but Fall"

Roi Faineant (online), September 2022
"inside the lip"

Vagabond City Lit (online), March 2023
"Sapphic Stanza 3"

Re-Verb (online), May 2023
"Love Poem for Laura #4, 2009"

Sinister Wisdom, April 2024
"Wild and Frail and Beautiful"

California Quarterly, summer 2024
"The Last Third, Denver to Santa Fe"

Bless all human beings who recognize, praise, and encourage poets, especially teachers, in my case, from grade school through graduate school—1st grade: Grace Anderson; 4th grade: Susan Donowitz and Beverly Baio; 5th grade: Jaye Vedder; 10th grade and onward: Audre Allison (and guest poet Ron Overton), the late Jeff Bennett, Moia Joyner, Florence Mondry, and Judith Schutzman; college at the University at Buffalo: the late Robert Creeley, Alexis De Veaux, Irving Feldman, Susan Howe, Stacy Hubbard, and Deidre Lynch; at Warren Wilson College's MFA Program for Writers: Debra Allbery; and at Ohio University: J. Allyn Rosser, Carey Snyder, and Bianca Lynne Spriggs. I also want to thank Eileen Myles and their Henry Street Settlement workshop; Elise Paschen, who hired me as an intern at the Poetry Society of America, and Mei-mei Berssenbrugge, who, at a Santa Fe cocktail party, acknowledged and encouraged the poet in me when most others only saw a tired mother of two babies.

I am grateful to my beloveds and muses: my wife and cover designer, Laura M. André; my writing partner: essayist, poet, and cover pigeon artist, Anna Chotlos; my mother, Linda Shaw; my sister, Lisa Walsh; my chosen brother, David Bedrick; my cousins, Tara Donnelly Moylan and Kristieanne Karlson; and my previous spouse and lifelong friend, Peter Gaugy, and our children, Honorée and Nathaniel.

I've been blessed with an embarrassment of riches when it comes to writer friends. A special thanks to Emily Axelrod, Rachel Aydt, Michelle Baker, Dalanie Beach, Nicole Chvatal, Leah De Forest, Anne Elliott, Michael Feigin, Jason Galloway, Tom Hespos, Ann marie Houghtailing, Samantha Imperi, Annabella Johnson, Ana June, Rozella Kennedy, Pietje Kobus, Denise LaCongo, Rose Levy Beranbaum, Pam Mayer, Melissa Mendonca, Alyson Mosquera Dutemple, Chris Nelson, Theo Pauline Nestor, Hieu Minh Nguyen, Melanie Ritzenthaler, Cassie Premo Steele, Tanya Taylor Rubinstein, and Austin Tucker.

I remain deeply grateful to the editors who selected my poems for publication: April Bradford, Aaron Burch, Edward Cohen, Angela Derain, Clair Dunlap, Julie R. Enszer, Ariel Gore, Samara Landau, Ian MacMenamin, Liz Mayer, Lindsey Medina, Emma McNamara, Miriam Sagan, Nicholas Skaldetvind, Gal Slonim, Tiffany M. Storrs, and Claire Waldrop. Most significantly, I thank Yellow Arrow Publishing editor-in-chief Kapua Iao and her brilliant team: Sydney Alexander, Marylou Fusco, Caroline Kunz, Alexa Laharty, Melissa Nunez, Ann Quinn, Mel Silberger, and Beck Snyder.

CANDACE WALSH holds a PhD in English (creative writing) from Ohio University and an MFA in fiction from Warren Wilson College. She was appointed visiting assistant professor of English at Ohio University for the 2024/25 academic year. Recent publication credits include, for poetry, *California Quarterly*, *Sinister Wisdom*, *Vagabond City Lit*, and *HAD*; for fiction, *The Greensboro Review*, *Passengers Journal*, and *Leon Literary Review*; and for creative nonfiction, *March Danceness*, *New Limestone Review*, and *Pigeon Pages*. Her craft essays and book reviews have appeared in *Brevity*, *descant*, *New Mexico Magazine*, and *Fiction Writers Review*. She is currently working on a novel and a craft essay collection. Find her on Twitter, Instagram, and Facebook @candacewalsh; her website is candacewalsh.com.

Thank you for supporting independent publishing.

Yellow Arrow Publishing is a nonprofit supporting writers and artists identifying as women. Visit YellowArrowPublishing.com for information on our publications, workshops, and writing opportunities.

www.ingramcontent.com/pod-product-compliance
Lightning Source LLC
LaVergne TN
LVHW041224080526
838199LV00083B/3297